EZ READERS
AN IMPRINT OF
MITCHELL LANE PUBLISHERS

CREATING YOUNG NONFICTION READERS

EZ Readers offer nonfiction for beginning readers in PreK through first grade, using simple language, clear illustrations, and engaging facts to build vocabulary and confidence.

TIPS FOR READING NONFICTION WITH BEGINNING READERS

Talk about Nonfiction

Begin by explaining that nonfiction books give us information that is true. The book will be organized around a specific topic or idea, and we may learn new facts through reading.

Look at the Parts

Most nonfiction books have helpful features. Our *EZ Readers* include color photographs and graphic aids, a table of contents, a glossary, and an index. Share the purpose of these features with your reader.

Color Photos and Graphic Aids

A lot of information can be found by "reading" photos, charts, maps, and other graphic aids found within nonfiction texts. Help your reader learn more about the different ways information can be displayed.

Table of Contents

Located at the front of the book, this list shows the big ideas within the text and the page numbers where they can be found.

Glossary

Located at the back of the book, the glossary defines key words and phrases that are related to the topic. These words and phrases can be found in the text in colored type.

Index

Located at the back of the book, an index is an alphabetical list of topics and the page numbers where they can be found.

With a little help and guidance about reading nonfiction, you can feel good about introducing a young reader to the world of *EZ Readers* nonfiction books.

EZ Readers is an imprint of:

Mitchell Lane
PUBLISHERS

2001 SW 31st Avenue
Hallandale, FL 33009
mitchelllanepub.com

First Edition, 2027.

Author: Meg Greve
Designer: Rhea Magaro
Editor: Kim Thompson

Library of Congress Cataloging-in-Publication Data
Title: A Day in the Life of a Lunch Box / by Meg Greve

Description: Hallandale, FL :
Mitchell Lane Publishers, [2027]

Identifiers:
ISBN 979-8-89260-845-9 (library bound)
ISBN 979-8-89260-935-7 (eBook)

Library of Congress Control Number: 2025950830

PHOTO CREDITS
Dreamstime: Ankevanwyk, 18; Shutterstock: Yash2rushter, 1; Viktorija Reuta, 1; 3DMI, 5, 22; Casezy idea, 5, 22; Mega Pixel, 5; Pixel-Shot, 7; reriyadi, 8; yulyamade, 10; sweet marshmallow, 10, 22; Inspiration GP, 13; 5House, 14; xpixel, 19, 22; Pixel-Shot, 21; Inspiration GP, 22; stockcreations, 22; 5House, 22; Olena Ivanova, 22.

Table of Contents

I Am a Lunch Box

I have a **handle**.

I have a zipper or a flap.

BY THE WAY...
I may be your favorite color. I may have your favorite character on me.

Good morning!

I am packed.

I slept in the **fridge**.
(Brrr!)

Remember to grab me on your way to school.

BY THE WAY...
Some kids pack me in the morning.

BY THE WAY...

Is it lunchtime yet?
I cannot wait!

I wait for you all morning.

I do my job.

I keep your food fresh.

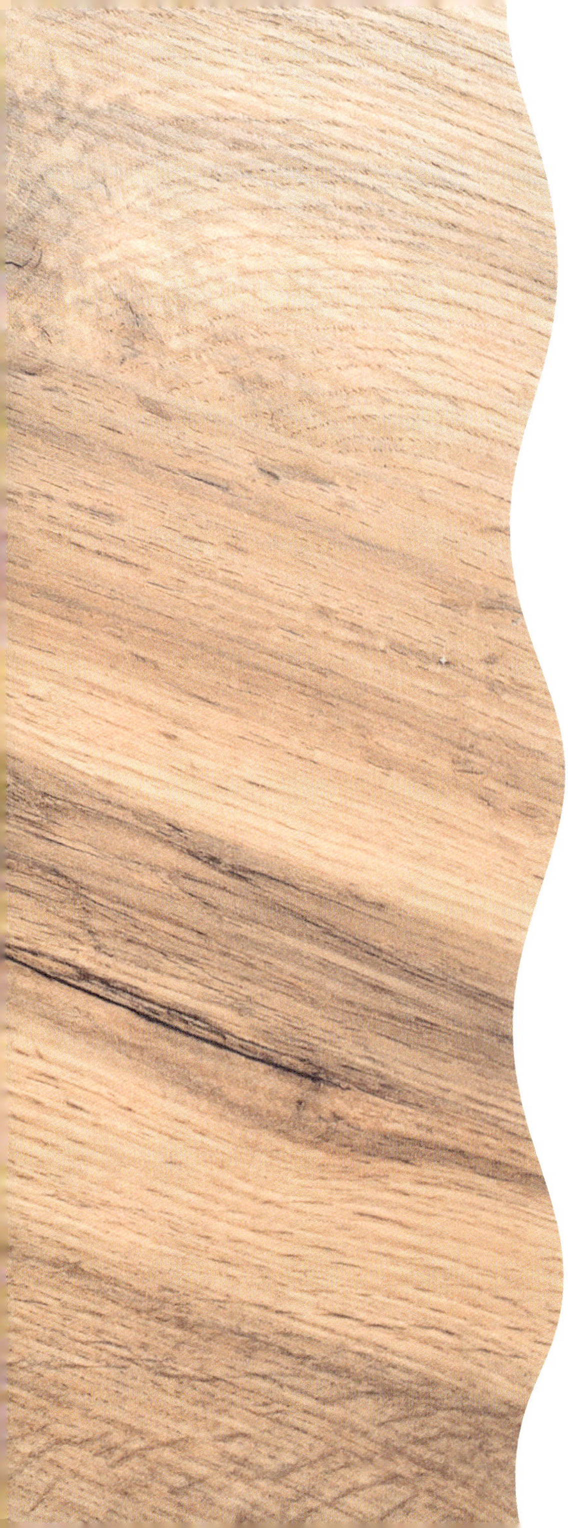

What is packed in me today?

Meat, nuts, or eggs?

Cheese, yogurt, or milk?

Peaches or grapes? Carrots or broccoli?

Bread or crackers?

By the way...

Fruits and veggies are full of vitamins. Grains give you energy.

I hope there is a sweet **treat**.

If it is jelly, I am *jam-packed*!

(See? I made a joke!)

It is lunchtime.
(Finally!)

You pop me open.

You crunch and
munch.

By the way...
When you get home, give me a good scrub!

I have trash. Yuck!
Throw it away!

I have **crumbs**. Eww!
Shake them out!

I do not like to be messy.

After school, please put me in the kitchen.

I will wait to get packed again.

BY THE WAY...
See you tomorrow!

Glossary

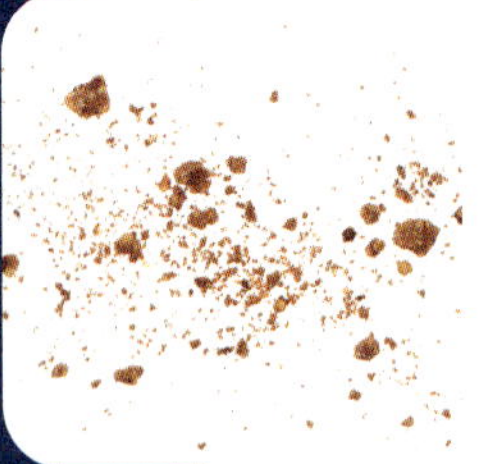

crumbs (kruhmz) little pieces of leftover food

dairy (DAIR-ee) a type of food that is made from milk and that helps build teeth and bones

fridge (frig) short for *refrigerator*; a machine that keeps things cold

grains (graynz) plants used to make bread and cereal, such as wheat and oats

handle (HAN-duhl) the part of an object that helps you carry it

protein (PROH-teen) a nutrient found in meat and eggs that helps build muscle

treat (treet) a food that is usually sweet and that is not eaten often or in large quantities

veggies (VE-jeez) vegetables such as broccoli, spinach, and carrots

Quiz Me

1. I eat protein and dairy foods for lunch.

   A. Yes B. No

2. I eat grains for lunch.

   A. Yes B. No

3. I eat fruits and vegetables for lunch.

   A. Yes B. No

4. I clean out my lunch box.

   A. Yes B. No

ANSWER KEY:

How many times did you answer yes?

4: Awesome! You know how to pack a healthy lunch.

3: Great! Your lunches are good for you.

2: That's okay! Keep learning and practicing.

1: You're starting to learn. Keep trying!

Further Reading

Peter Pauper Press. *Would You Rather? Lunch Box Notes.* Peter Pauper Press, 2025.

Taste of Home, ed. *Kids Can Cook!* Trusted Media Brands, 2025.

On the Internet

Eating Well: The Top 10 Healthiest Foods for Kids

eatingwell.com/article/291139/the-top-10-healthiest-foods-for-kids

Find out what foods are both healthy and tasty.

USDA: My Plate

myplate4chatbot.stg.platform.usda.gov/life-stages/kids

Find apps, games, and activities to help you fill your plate with healthy foods.

Index

About the Author

Meg Greve has been in education for more than 30 years. She is a mom of two kids who used to love a healthy lunch like peanut butter and jelly, carrot sticks, and yogurt. Sometimes, lunch got packed in a brown bag when they forgot their lunch boxes at school!